My First Seashores

Nature Activity Book

James Kavanagh
Illustrations by Raymond Leung
and Steve Patton

Printed in China. For further information, contact Waterford Press Inc., 1123 Overcash Dr., Dunedin, FL 34698.
To order, call 800-434-2555; Fax: 727-330-7765. To share comments, email us at editor@waterfordpress.com
For information on custom-published products, call 800-434-2555.
ISBN: 978-158355-590-3

WORD SEARCH

Find the letters that spell the names of these fishes.

FLOUNDER

SCULPIN

HERRING

C	Q	W	G	H	C	Y	I	I	M
P	I	P	E	F	I	S	H	D	Y
S	A	N	D	L	A	N	C	E	P
Q	M	G	J	O	C	H	Z	I	L
Y	B	C	C	U	G	D	P	Z	N
B	Q	K	I	N	E	F	Q	V	V
P	R	F	O	D	G	B	I	V	Q
Q	D	X	D	E	Q	G	V	S	I
Z	H	E	R	R	I	N	G	S	H
S	C	U	L	P	I	N	R	P	K

PIPEFISH

SAND LANCE

DOGFISH

answers

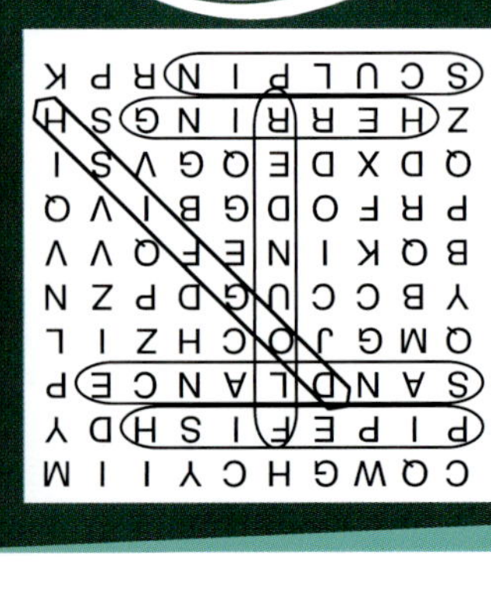

WHO AM I?

Draw a line between the seashore plant and its name.

1. 

2. 

3. 

4. 

Kelp

Grass

Cactus

Palm

answers 1. Cactus 2. Palm 3. Kelp 4. Grass

CONNECT THE DOTS

I can be seen swimming behind boats and jumping into the air.

Who am I?

answer Dolphin

SHADOW KNOW-HOW

Can you identify these marine mammals?

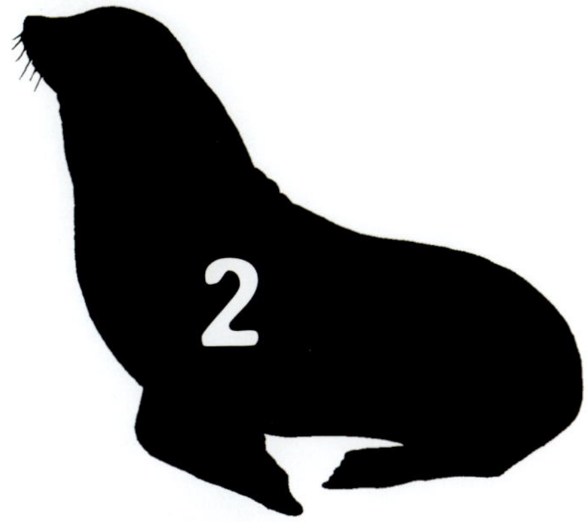

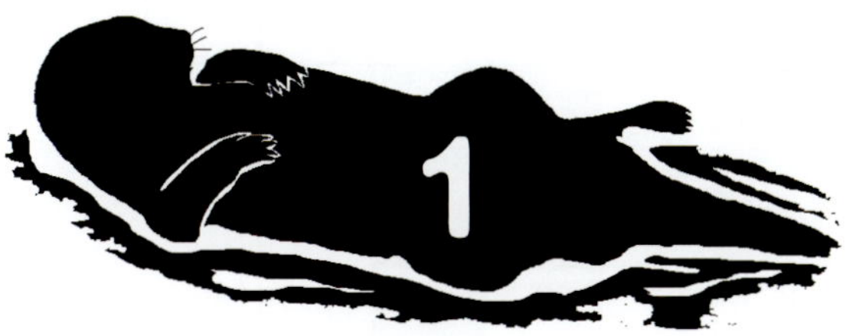

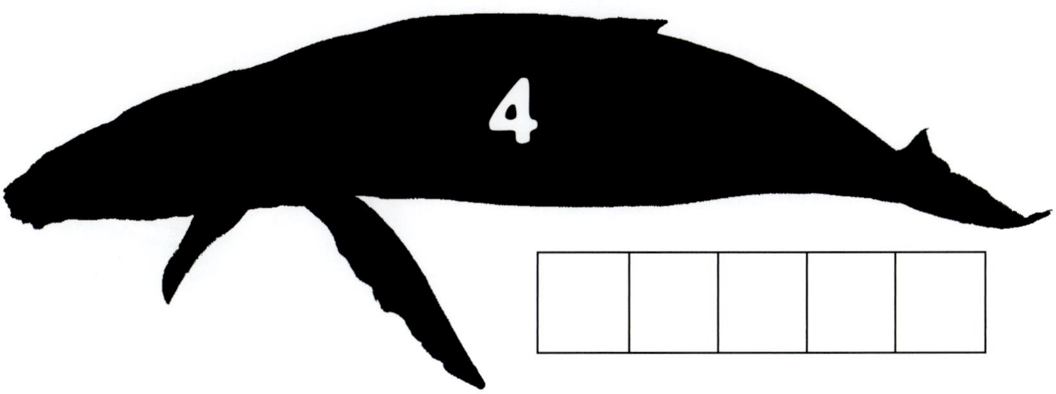

answers

1. Sea Otter
2. Seal
3. Dolphin
4. Whale

CROSSWORD

Across

1. I have a shell. 
2. I am named for my shape. 
3. I am a sea _ _ _ _. 
4. I am a squishy _ _ _ _ _ fish. 

Down

2. I often bask on the shore. 
5. I am as big as a _ _ _ _ _. 
6. I am tiny as a _ _ _ _ _ _ _. 
7. I am a _ _ _ _ _ _ _ whale. 

MAKE WORDS

The **bluehead**
is a reef fish common
in tropical waters.

How many words can you make from the letters in its name?

______________________ ______________________

______________________ ______________________

______________________ ______________________

______________________ ______________________

______________________ ______________________

______________________ ______________________

answers

Possible answers include: be, he, ad, ale, ade, lee, bed, bad, bud, led, eel, dab, dub, deal, blue, head, heed, lead, bead, dale, bale, hale, lube, heel, bleed

WHO AM I?

Draw a line between the fish and its name.

1. 

2. 

3. 

4. 

Shark

Swordfish

Flounder

Ray

answers

1. Swordfish
2. Ray
3. Shark
4. Flounder

Be an Artist

Draw this sea turtle by copying it one square at a time.

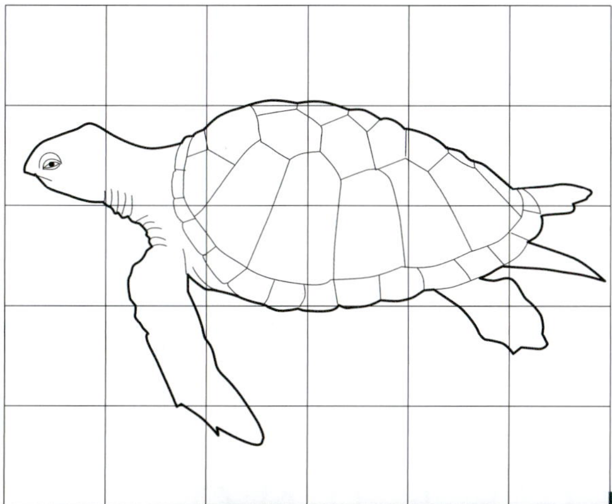

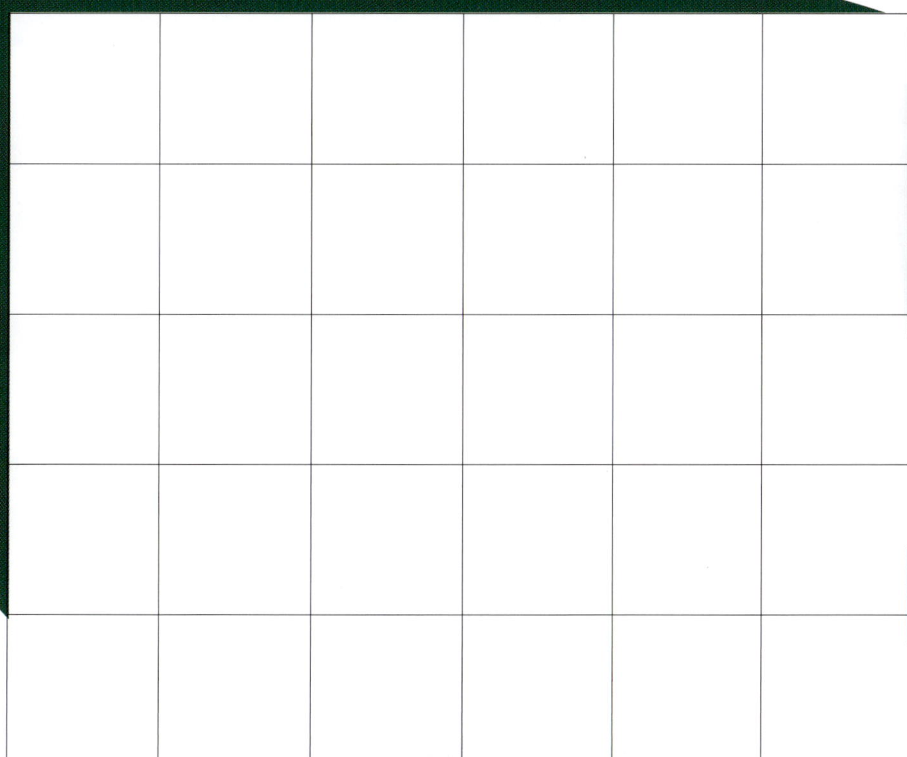

WORD SEARCH

Seashore Plants

O	S	Z	H	I	I	Z	D	N	I
U	E	X	H	F	I	D	V	U	Y
T	A	P	B	N	W	D	B	R	M
O	G	R	Q	A	M	V	E	H	K
Q	R	I	E	W	M	X	A	Y	L
S	A	M	Z	E	A	B	C	S	V
G	P	R	Y	V	D	F	H	D	S
C	E	O	N	E	N	H	P	Y	T
I	G	S	H	D	N	Q	E	W	O
J	V	E	R	B	E	N	A	J	I

SEA GRAPE

REED

BEACH PEA

VERBENA

PRIMROSE

answers

COLOR ME

Anemone

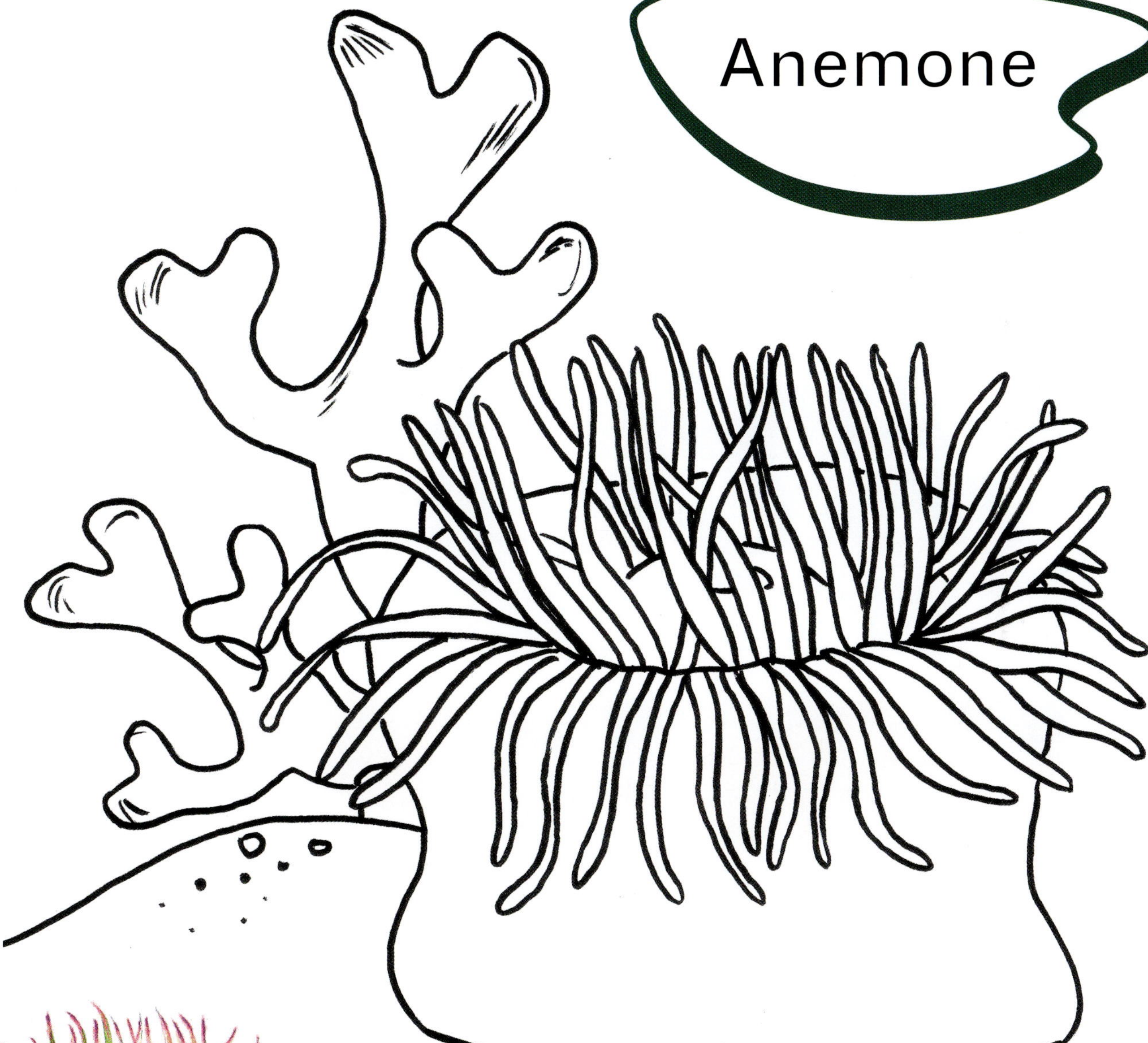

color key

ORIGAMI

Starting with a square piece of paper, follow the folding instructions below to create this whale.

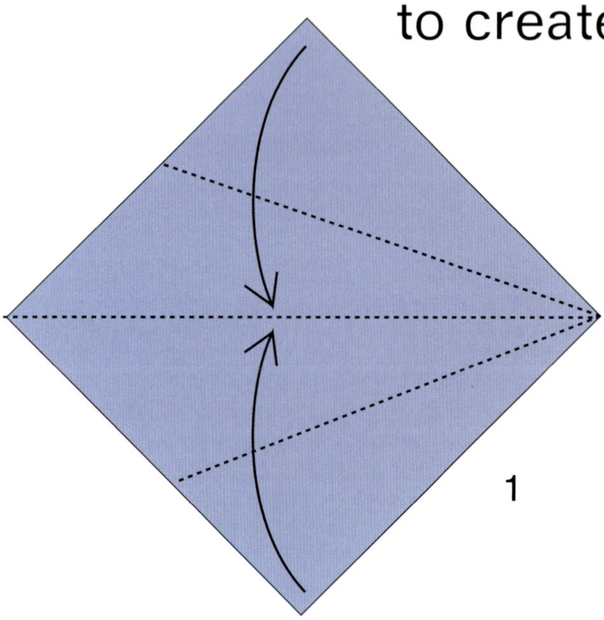

1

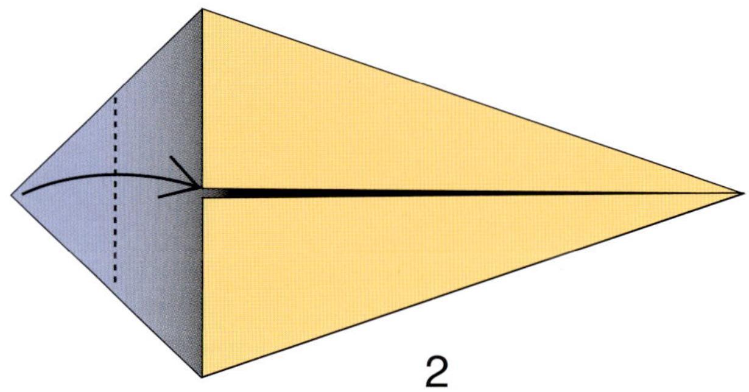

2

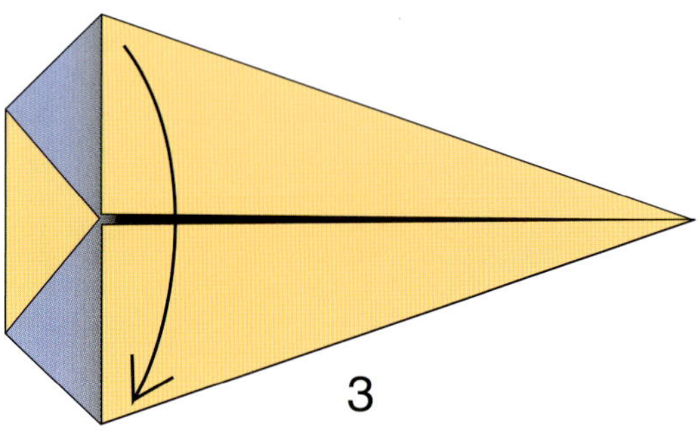

3

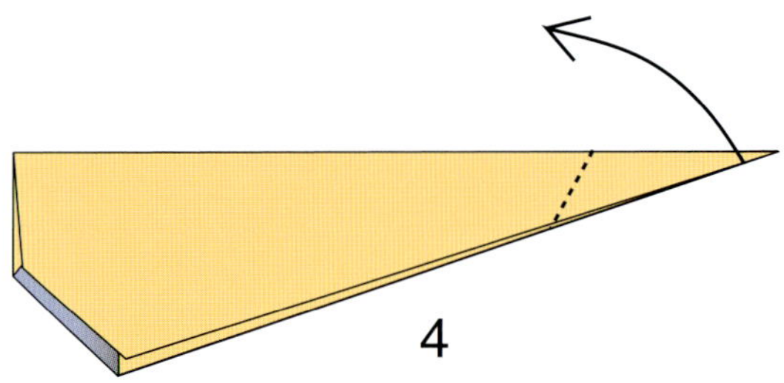

4

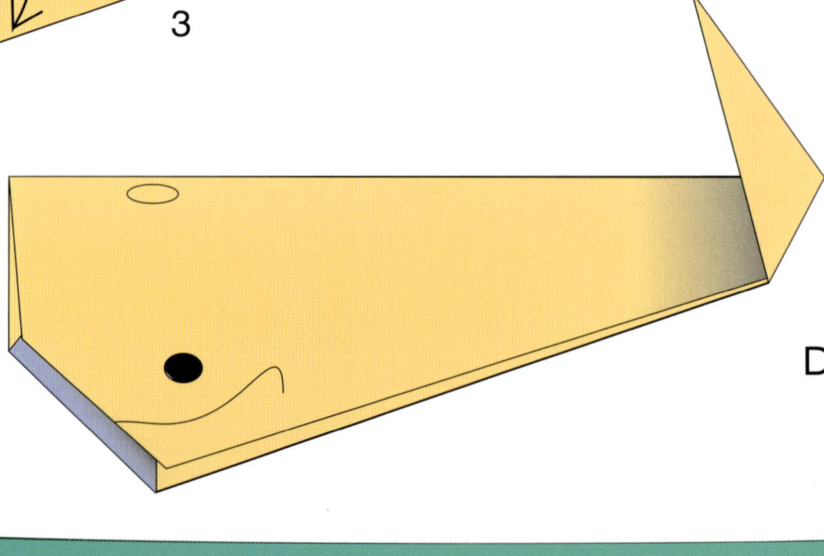

Draw its eye, mouth and blowhole.

Maze

Triggerfish travel in large groups called "schools" and feed near reefs and rocks. Help this triggerfish find its school.

NAME SCRAMBLE

Unscramble the names of these seashore animals.

1.

h i f s

2.

a b r c

3.

u c d k

4.

l a s e

answers

1. Fish
2. Crab
3. Duck
4. Seal

ODDBALL OUT

In each row, circle the seashore creature which is different from the others.

1.

1A

1B

1C

Two of these are crabs, one is not.

2.

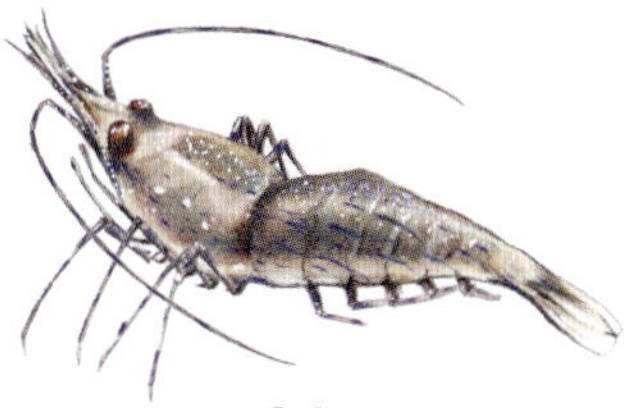

2A

2B

2C

Two of these are sea urchins, one is not.

3.

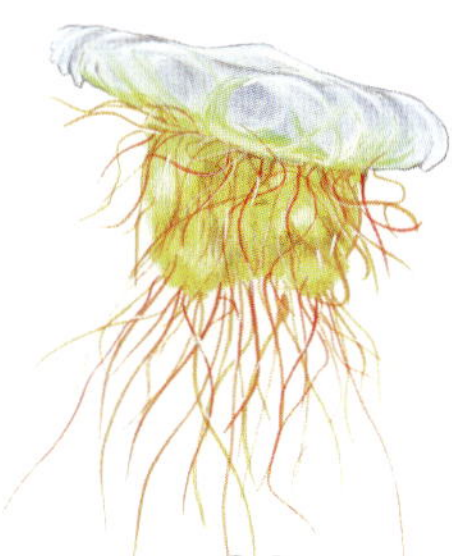

3A

3B

3C

Two of these are jellyfish, one is not.

answers

1. 1B is a shell
2. 2A is a shrimp
3. 3C is a sea star

FOOD CHAIN

Draw a line between the species and its place in the food chain.

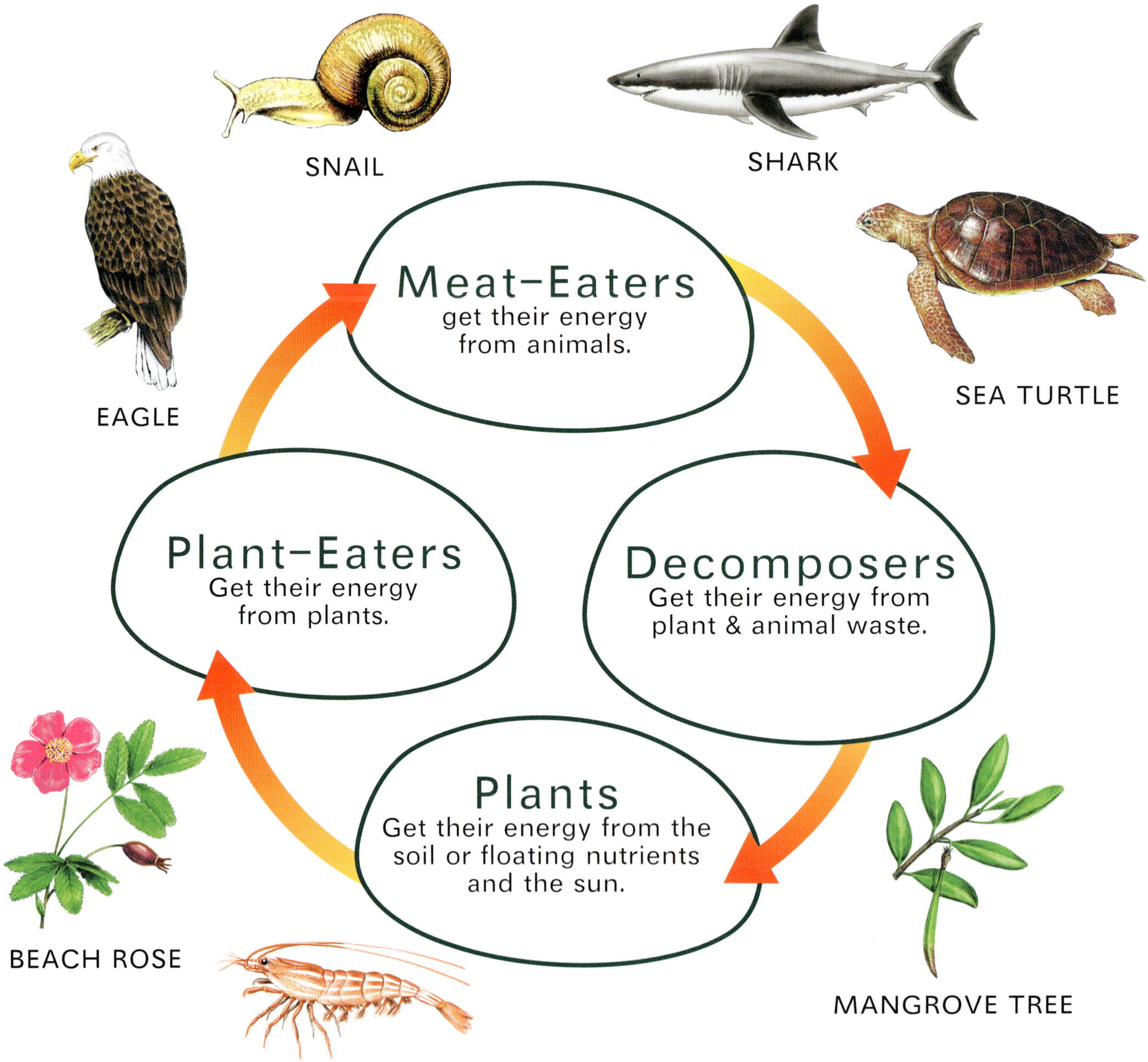

answers

Plants: beach rose, mangrove tree
Decomposers: shrimp, snail
Meat-eaters: eagle, shark
Plant-eaters: sea turtle

WHO AM I?

Draw a line between the seashore animal and its name.

1. 

2. 

3. 

4. 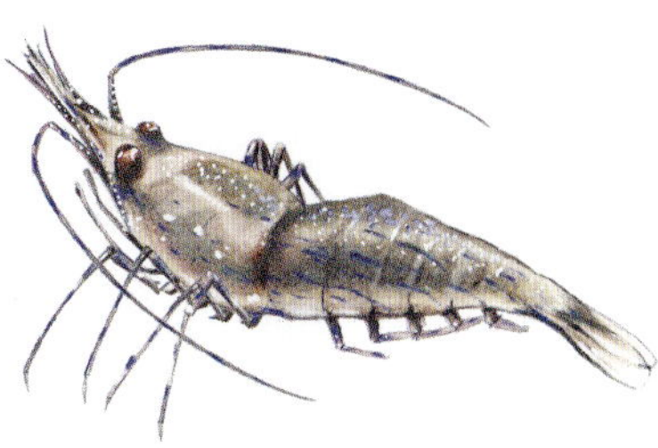

Jellyfish

Shrimp

Clam

Sea Star

answers

1. Clam
2. Jellyfish
3. Sea Star
4. Shrimp

WORD SEARCH

Seashore Birds

TERN

SEA GULL

SANDERLING

CURLEW

V S C Z S G N Q Q S

Y K U U D P B O E A

A F R Q O W W R E N

K J L R G W Y B V D

G S E A G U L L F E

J H W I L L E T K R

T H T Q P R X I Z L

P E R G M S G J L I

K F R I L R I N B N

J N H N N J O V R G

WILLET

answers

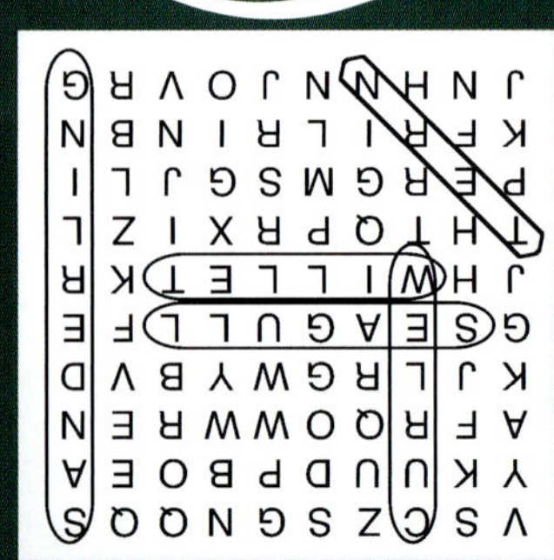

SHADOW KNOW-HOW

Can you identify these saltwater animals?

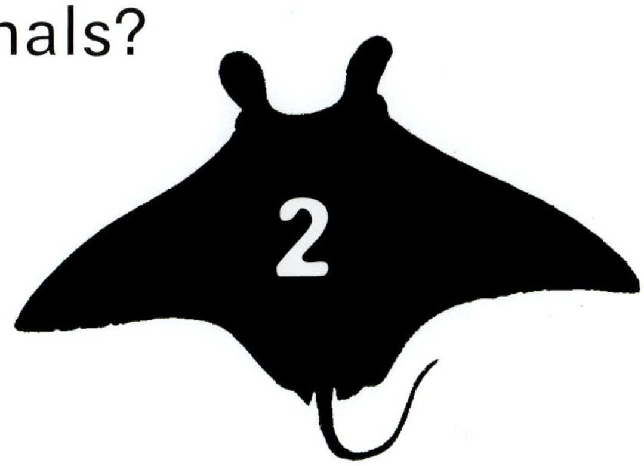

answers

1. Shark
2. Ray
3. Sea Horse
4. Whale
5. Swordfish

SPOT THE DIFFERENCES

Can you spot five differences between the whale pictures?

answers

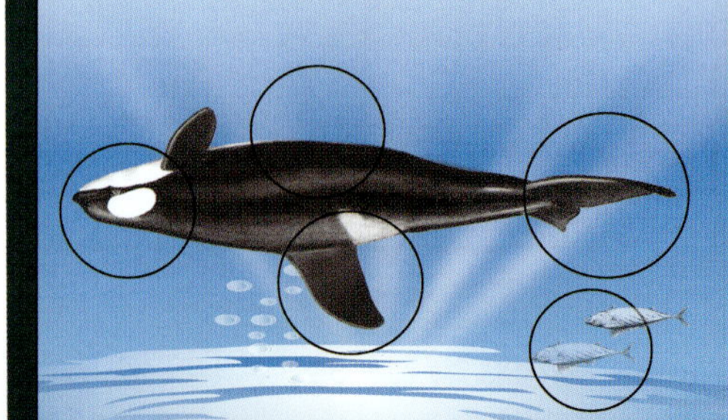

COLOR ME

Triggerfish

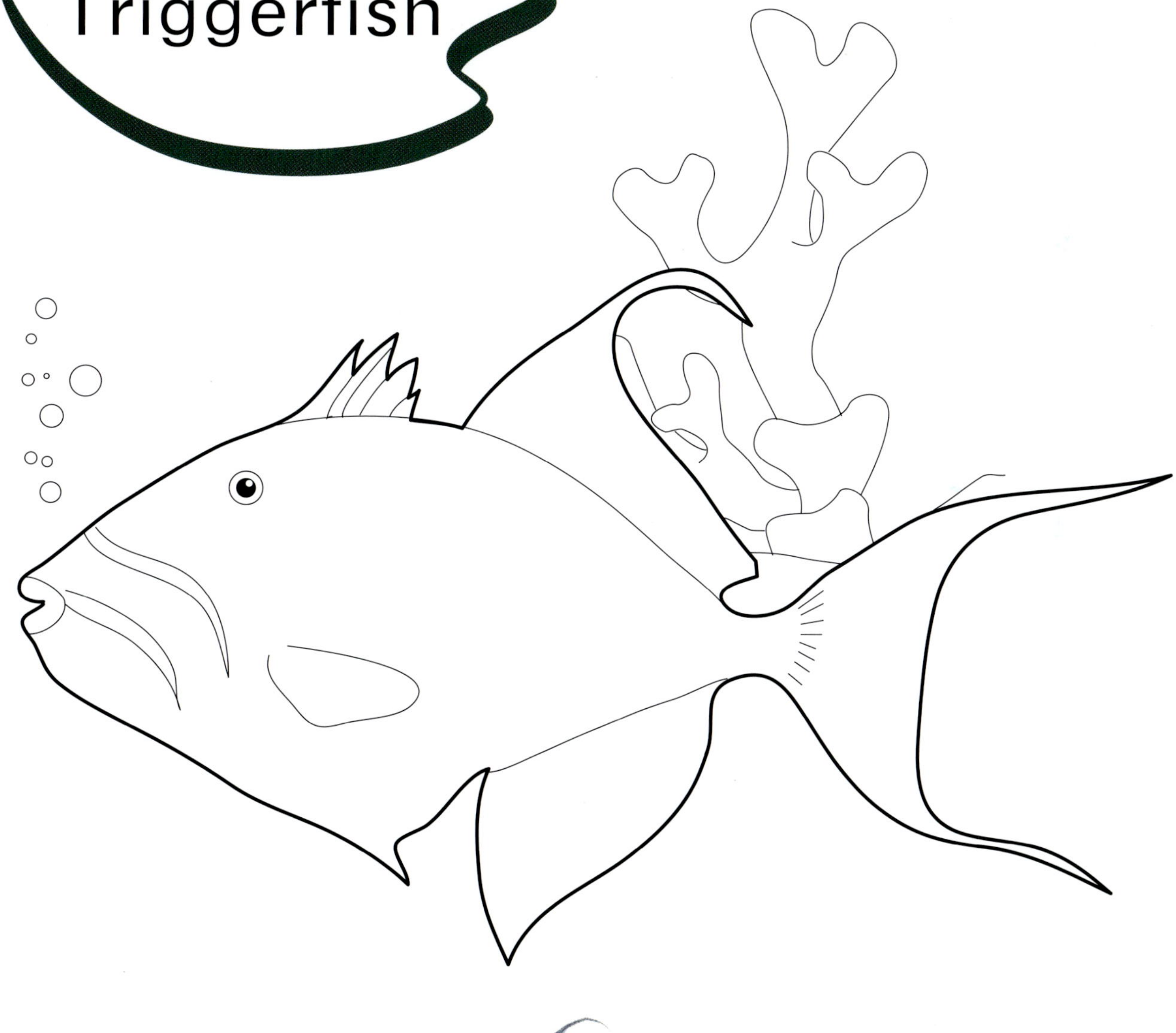

color key

CONNECT THE DOTS

I am often found in tidepools.
I hold onto rocks with tiny
suction cups on my ‘arms’.

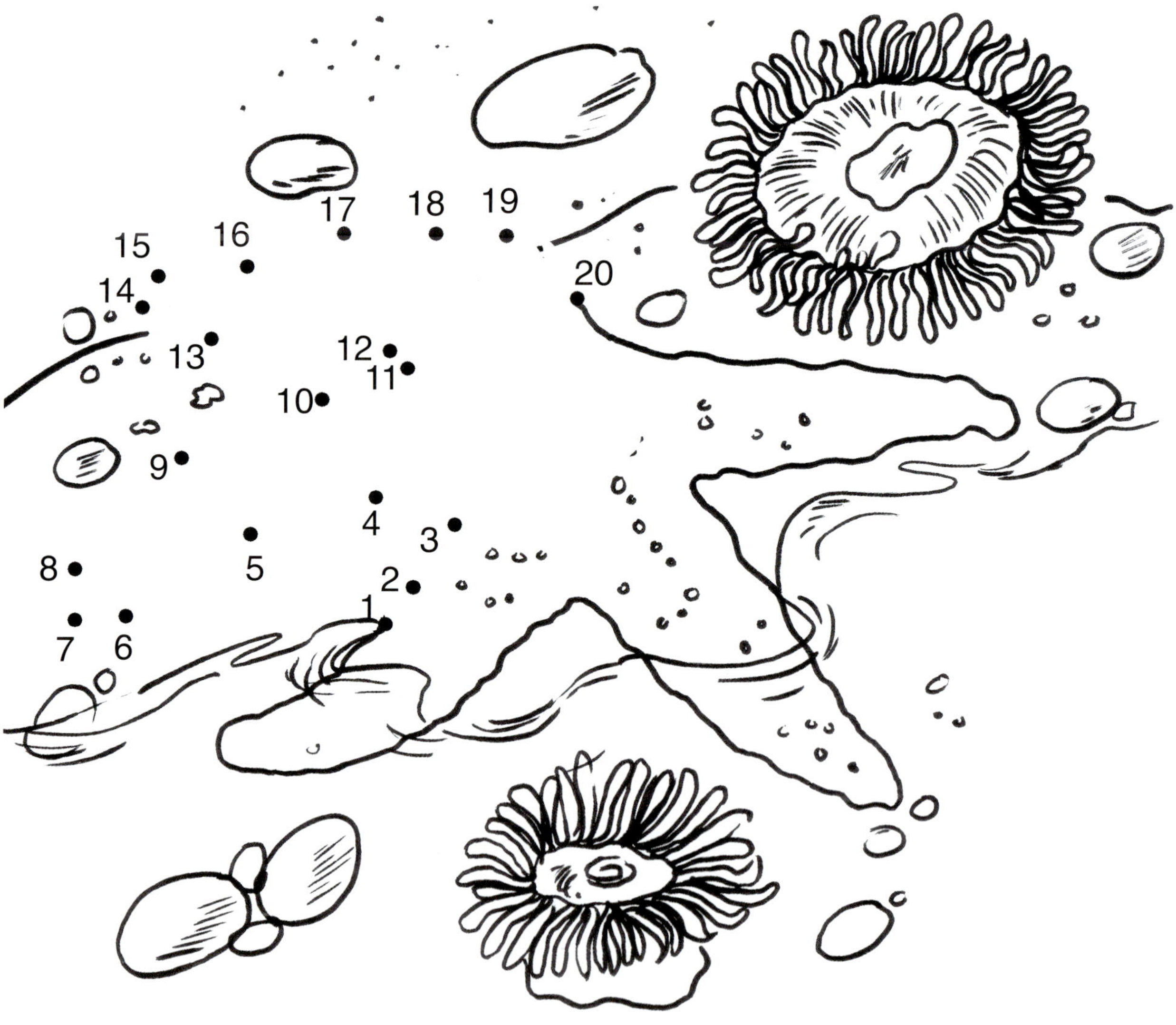

Who am I?

answer Sea star

MAKE WORDS

The **octopus** has eight limbs lined with suction cups that allow it to grasp its prey.

How many words can you make from the letters in its name?

answers

Possible answers include: so, to, top, tops, sop, sot, cot, cots, cop, cops, cut, cuts, pot, pots, pus, coot, coots, coop, coops, soot, stop, pout, pouts

Be an Artist

Draw this crab by copying it one square at a time.

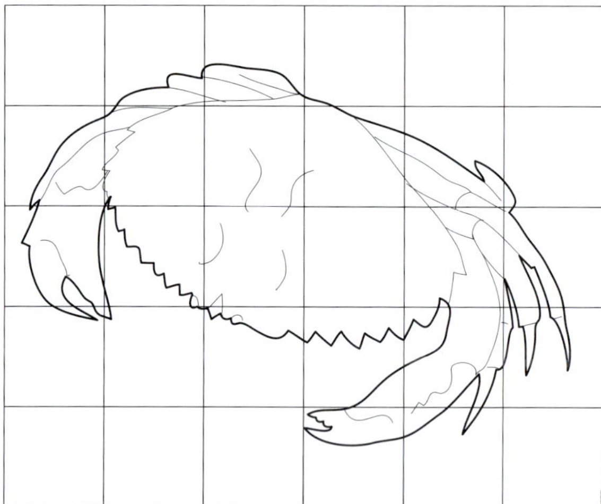

CLASS ACT

Draw a line between the animal and the group it belongs to.

SEA OTTER

Mammals

SEA TURTLE

SNAPPER

Birds

BASS

GULL

Reptiles

PELICAN

SEA LION

Fishes

WHALE

answers

Mammals – Sea Otter, Sea Lion, Whale

Birds – Gull, Pelican

Reptiles – Sea Turtle

Fishes – Snapper, Bass

WORD SEARCH

Marine Mammals

SEAL

OTTER

DOLPHIN

X	M	Z	Z	N	X	Z	Z	Y	G
A	E	G	S	P	N	A	D	B	O
X	G	E	R	J	K	Q	R	Y	X
Q	V	S	D	O	L	P	H	I	N
C	X	S	E	A	L	J	C	N	Q
O	G	N	S	A	J	U	Z	B	Z
A	T	W	H	A	L	E	E	E	W
D	E	T	W	N	E	I	I	R	R
K	N	L	E	X	Z	A	O	B	W
G	S	S	I	R	D	J	G	N	W

WHALE

SEA LION

answers

HOME SWEET HOME

Animals live where they can find food and a place to rest. Draw a line between the animal and its habitat.

1. 

SANDPIPER

2. 

SEA STAR

3. 

SHARK

4. 

CRAB

(a) 

A rocky tidepool is where to find this 5-limbed creature.

(b) 

This pinching seashore animal can be found hiding under rocks.

(c) 

This tiny bird is often seen running in and out with waves along seashores.

(d) 

This fearsome predator lives in the open ocean.

answers 1. (c) 2. (a) 3. (d) 4. (b)

WHO AM I?

Draw a line between the bird and its name.

1. 

2. 

3. 

4. 

Duck

Heron

Pelican

Gull

answers

1. Gull
2. Pelican
3. Duck
4. Heron

Maze

Can you help the hermit crab find a new shell to move into?

SPOT THE DIFFERENCES

Can you spot five differences
between the crabs?

answers

ODDBALL OUT

In each row, circle the animal which is different from the others.

1.

1A

1B

1C

Two of these are birds, one is not.

2.

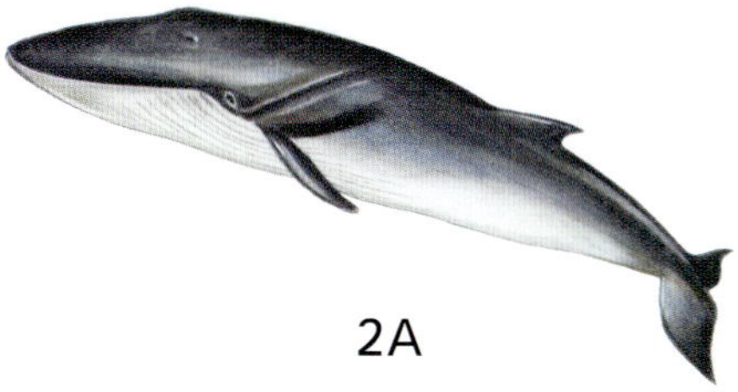

2A

2B

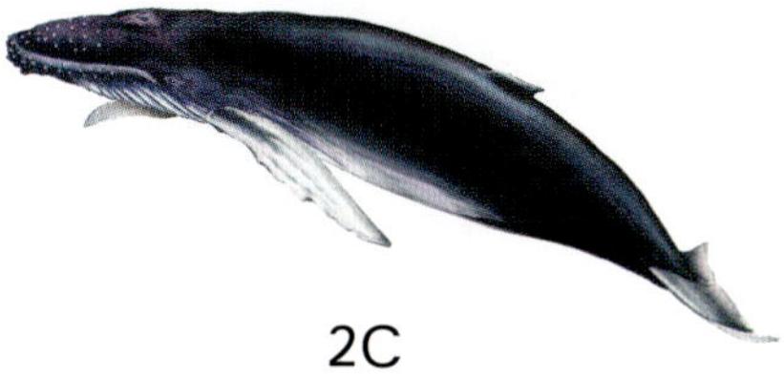

2C

Two of these are whales, one is not.

3.

3A

3B

3C

Two of these are sea mammals, one is not.

answers

1. 1A is a turtle
2. 2B is a fish
3. 3B is a bird

WORD SEARCH

Seashore Life

CORAL

STARFISH

L	A	K	C	R	T	R	B	P	L
J	S	D	O	S	E	A	P	E	N
S	E	T	R	S	R	F	T	P	C
W	A	L	A	K	I	A	G	J	Z
L	U	S	L	R	S	I	G	T	Z
O	R	H	M	Y	F	V	D	V	O
D	C	H	S	W	F	I	S	Y	W
H	H	X	N	A	U	I	S	Z	D
H	I	C	W	F	B	U	S	H	K
F	N	T	C	B	F	P	H	H	W

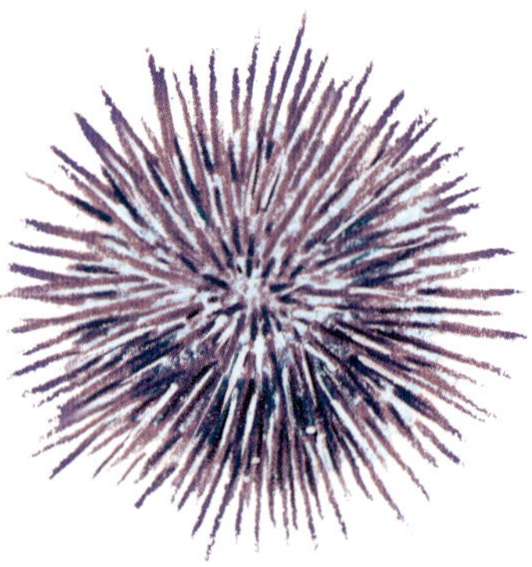

SEA URCHIN

SEA PEN

JELLYFISH

answer